Write the Book that Builds the Brand

Julia A. Royston

BK Royston Publishing
Jeffersonville IN
http://bkroystonpublishing.com
bkroystonpublishing@gmail.com

© 2023

All Rights Reserved. No part of this book may be reproduced, stored in a retrieval system, or transmitted by any means without the written permission of the author.

Cover and Layout: Elite Book Covers

ISBN-13: 978-1-959543-79-4

Printed in the United States of America

Dedication

I dedicate this book to every business owner no matter the industry. You have experience. You have expertise. You have a perspective. Let the world know it and put your stamp on the market with your own brand book.

Acknowledgements

I thank my Lord and Savior Jesus Christ for giving me another opportunity to introduce more people to you. I thank you that you have for entrusting this gift to me. Lord, let your Spirit move, guide and empower through this book the people who will read it.

To my husband, Brian K. Royston, the love of my life for loving and cheering me on so much that I can be and do all that God has placed in me. I love you.

To my Mom, my greatest supporter and best friend. To my Dad, who is in heaven, whom I know is proud of me and always encouraged me to go for it. Thanks to all the rest of my family for their love and support.

A special thank you to Rev. and Mrs. Claude R. Royston for their love and support.

To the rest of my clients, friends and family, thank you and love you always. Let's go!

Love, Julia

Table of Contents

Dedication	iii
Acknowledgements	v
Introduction	ix
Brand Book Definition	1
Uses for a Brand Book	11
Support Actions with a Brand Book	29
What Type of Book Does Your Brand Need?	43
Brand Book Outline	53
The Look of the Book	73
The End Game	81
About the Author	89
Other Books by Julia Royston	91

Introduction

If you are a business owner, coach, speaker or non-profit leader, thank you for purchasing and reading this book. I wrote this book with you in mind. Hopefully, you have written a book or even written a chapter in a book for the experience and expertise before we dive into this Brand Book process. If not, I highly recommend that you, purchase my, "Write that Book Now Book and Workbook" or "Idea Think Create" at www.juliaroystonstore.com to begin the process of writing your own book. These resources will help you to organize your thoughts and ideas along with making sure that you have a streamlined process for the book that you intend to write.

To date, I have written 85+ books. I say 85+ because I am always writing and probably will reach 100 books or more prior to complete retirement or death. I write because I love the creative process, for me, it is therapeutic and healing to write and I write because my clients need something or I want to teach something and refer to my own book or there is a need in the marketplace.

I was asked to speak about "The Power of the Brand Book." For me it is all about writing the Book to Build or in Direct Alignment With Your Brand. It is a great topic. I find that people are writing books that don't start, build or expand their brand and therefore, people are not drawn to them or their business. Their book gets lost and just becomes another book on Amazon which can easily overlooked given the number of books on that platform. This statement is in no wise shade as the young people say or discount of anyone's book that is already published. It's just the truth and when it comes to sales there are little to no sales. I have experienced first-hand the disappointment of low sales with a book but quickly go back to the drawing board. I will revisit or change the cover or more promotion or finally, realizing that it was the timing of release or I just hadn't found an audience for that book. I have written books because I wanted to, thought it was a great idea and/or loved the fictional characters. But, when it is time for a book that speaks directly to and for my brand, I'm careful, strategic and all in.

Turn the page and let's go!

Brand Book Definition

I salute and know that there are other brand specialists out there that may have a different definition of branding. But, I want to give you my definition of brand and/or branding.

A brand is a mark of accomplishment, level of expertise, product, service or experience you have with a person, place, product or event. The #1 reflection of the brand is you, the owner, inventory, promoter, etc. No matter the colors, logo, emblem, signs, product or service, it is a reflection of you. What do people get when they get you? What do people come away with when they work with you? How do you make people feel, learn and grow when they work with you? Whether people lie or don't put in the work, there should be someone else who can say, "I don't know about your experience, but I had a great experience when I worked with…, used that product or purchased that service." There could be a person out there who says, "We couldn't work together so she refunded my money or sent me a comparable product to replace the one that was damaged or just said no and referred me to someone who could help me."

For me, these are a reflection of my personal brand and my business brand. Some people don't care about either. They are just trying to make money any way that they can or as the young people say, "get the bag." For me, that doesn't work. My father taught me that "a good name is all you have and should be chosen more than great riches." I also know from personal experience that people talk about you and your business and often refer people to you and you don't even know them. I was recently at an event and smiled and said, "good morning." The lady said, "I already know about you and coming back to buy some books from you. You are Julia 'A' Royston and not just Julia Royston." I thought, "Who was that and how did she know about me, especially putting the A as my middle initial?" Needless to say, I was on my toes the entire time. She came back, too. But whether people say, "Do you know Julia A. Royston?" or whether people say, "do you know about BK Royston Publishing?" they are speaking about your brand. Now your personal brand is about you as a person apart from your business. Your business brand is known by the logo, colors, symbol and — in my case — the books that they have purchased. I tried to separate the two and just focus on the logo without me representing it and/or putting a stock image of someone else on the advertisements and it didn't work. It may work for other brands, but it didn't work for me. People came back with, "Who is this lady?" or "Did you sell your company?" or "Who is running it now?" or "Did you go out of business?" It only took one time and I realized that didn't work. So for me, my personal brand (me) and my business brands (BK Royston Publishing or Royal Media and Publishing or Book Business Boss) are all tied together. After 15 years in business, I am not going to separate them but strengthen, build and expand them in the direction in which I am led.

Now before we move forward with the specifics of writing or the contents of a brand book, let me interject that a brand book can not only build your brand but be building blocks and elevate your platform, perspective and expertise in your particular industry and marketplace. Your brand book can support a specific platform or arm of your brand or the overall brand itself. I'll talk more about this later but the "Write, Publish and Promote Series" is a brand building book for all of publishing brands but also my writing coaching brand, Julia Royston Enterprises and my consulting brand, Book Business Boss. These books are platforms that I stand on to guide my clients to writing books, but there are also other books that guide my clients in their businesses and promotional opportunities and needs as well. There are some ministry leaders that if I named the book and not the person, you would know who wrote it because the book helped build and expand their brand as well as extended or raised their platform to cross over from being just related to their ministry to attaining a worldwide and global audience. That's a powerful book! Of course, that's not the only thing that propelled them to the next level: there was also branding, a team, marketing, promotion, public relations, positioning, production, performance, execution and God as well.

Writing a brand book is associated with your personal and business brands. If you need help, let's have a conversation. Schedule a call at www.talkwithroyston.com.

Take a minute and define what you think your brand strengths and weaknesses are.

_____

_____

_____

_____

_____

_____

_____

_____

_____

_____

_____

_____

_____

_____

Next ask someone else what they think your brand strengths and weaknesses are.

_____

_____

_____

_____

_____

_____

_____

_____

_____

_____

_____

_____

_____

_____

_____

_____

Finally, compare what you think and what others think of your brand.

Notes:

Uses for a Brand Book

Why do you need a brand book?

A brand book can be used in so many ways and I'll get more specific later in this chapter but, primarily there are a few reasons why you need a brand book.

1. Your brand is a part of an industry or area of business. With your book, it is going to be your perspective on the industry and your approach to that particular marketplace.
2. A brand book can be a reasonable entry or access point to doing business with you. You might have a high ticket-price item or package that is desirable but financially some people may not be ready to invest on

that level because they don't know you. Remember people do business with people they know, like and trust. They may be impressed with you but clearly don't know you yet, so a book—especially a brand book—is a way for people to be introduced to your brand and learn how to connect with your brand.

3. Books are "Evergreen." An Evergreen book is one that should not go out of style or should remain viable throughout any season of the year. The goal of any business should to be in business all year round for many years to come. Your brand book should be able to be read, utilized and implemented as precedent for business owners for years to come.

4. Finally, I have a hard time believing that you can be in business or be committed to an industry area for more than 10 years and have nothing to say, good or bad, about how your industry can be better or grow or teach the next generations and beyond.

How do you use a brand book?

I have given this example often. When I first went to work for a Fortune 500 company, as new hires they gave us two things: an appointment planner and the book's history. Both books were extremely important for me as an employee. The planner was to help me get organized and never miss an appointment or event so I could arrive on time. The history of the company book gave me the backstory of the company, how it got started, the evolution of the company, its principles, techniques, failures and successes. It was inspiring and informative to say the least. Now that was a brand book, but it was to do something different from what you might want your brand book to do. Their brand book gave not only the history but also the standards of doing business and working for that company. Sort of like a subversive handbook but not directly.

Your brand book may tell some of your backstory, history, failures, lessons and successes, but you want to draw the potential client closer in to know more about you and to ultimately, want to do business with you. On the other hand, the Fortune 500 company had the money, contacts, clients and successful brand already, they just needed me, the employee, to get on board, take it seriously, do the work and help push and grow the brand to the next level with excellence.

Not only can you have your brand book tell others about you, your main principles, history, etc., but it can prepare your client to work with you. For example, if you were in real estate, the documents, mindset, review of your budget, financials, etc., could be included in your brand book so that when they schedule the appointment, they are better prepared, the process can go more smoothly and the home can be acquired easier as well as the commission could come more quickly into your bank account.

I can honestly say, to date, that I have used something from all of my 86 books that I have written to support my brand. Whether it was writing style, formatting, instruction, presentations, etc., there is something that can assist, support and help the audience that I am speaking to from my books. My goal is always to not only build my brand but to also build the audience to implement and execute what I teach in their own books, businesses and brands.

With that said, the following is just a small list of ways that a brand book can be used or examples of how I have used my brand books. Whether you use the book as a standalone textbook or in conjunction with all of these different products, services or opportunities, create a brand book that will work for you, your business and brand.

We're going to use two of my books as an example: *Write, Publish and Promote that*

Book Now Series and *From Author to Entrepreneur.*

Writing Coaching, Lead Magnets and Workshops

The *Write that Book Now* book has been used so much it is not funny. I was so reluctant to even write the *Write, Publish and Promote* series but was encouraged by my good friend, Vanessa Collins. She told me that I needed a brand book, and I am glad I listened. At first, like me, you might think that the brand book will give too many of your business secrets away, but if you write it correctly, it will lead more people to you and, hopefully, turn into more clients.

Write that Book Now is a book to help people start, continue or finish their books. I have used it with workshops, lead magnets, coaching sessions as well as using any chapter or the whole book to assist a client. I have said it many times and will continue to say that a book is your content and intellectual property; you can use it any way that you see fit to help you, your client and overall brand.

Look at your book's chapter titles and see how you are helping a potential client, answering a question or solving a problem. That should be your main goal because otherwise, why do you need to purchase your book? Let's go!

Publishing Coaching and Workshops

There are those who actually want to self-publish their own books but what better way to help by giving them guidance to do it better, more easily and become a resource just in case they run into problems. I have taught a full 10-week publishing course in which I have used the book as well.

Even though someone may not buy one of my full publishing packages, I am still offering my services in a different way. It still brings people into my sphere of influence and hopefully, I can assist or upsell to another package or opportunity. It works, I promise you.

Book Promotion Workshops, Coaching and Published Author Resources

Now, when it comes to being a published author, the hardest part is promotion. I know you think that it's the writing or publishing but it's not; it's promotion. There are a lot of books out here so there is competition. I provide this *Promote that Book Now* as a published author resource for those I've published and those I did not publish. I have had book promotion workshops, masterclasses and included it in writing retreats and conferences. Now, you can see how this first series is so important to my business, to those in the world who want to do what I do, and it gets the basics, guidance and information on paper for the world to refer to. Additionally, this is told from my perspective and my experience in the publishing industry. I will always have this contribution to the industry no matter how much or how little I am recognized by others.

Finally, I take this series everywhere I go because I always have someone ask me or know somebody or want to gift this series to someone who is thinking about writing, publishing or promoting a book. I have seen people who have purchased my books to publish on their own, but I know that deep down that I made a contribution to that book project on some level.

My business coach always told us to have a small, medium, large and VIP way for people to work with us. The books are on the lower level to work with me at the cost of $10–15, but that cost is replicated over and over again. When you sell 20–50 of these books a month, those $10 or $15 dollar amounts can add up. Don't sleep on the book sales. It can help and turn into something else for your business and brand. Let's go!

Coaching Brand Book

Over time, I have assisted authors to turn their books into businesses. Primarily, these authors are asked by their supporters and future clients for more information, coaching, mentoring, etc. So there are several things that have to change including first and foremost the mindset of business owner instead of employment/worker mindset. If you know my background, I was raised by entrepreneurial parents, but my dad was bivocational as well. He was an educator in the daytime, and my mom ran the business while my dad was at work. Then we had a cleaning service with 50 employees in the evening. Now, I don't know about you, but 50 employees was a major business in my eyes. So I have seen "up close and personal" what being a business owner looks like. It is a lot of work and not for the faint of heart. Now, after nearly 16 years of my business, with the last 5 years full-time, I have much to say about this subject.

Make this transition into business from just having a book is a great guide for any new author and business owner. In addition, I also take the book apart and slice it into smaller pieces so that people can digest it better or approach the process step by step.

Supplement for the Brand Book

Once you get started helping people, they'll have more questions and they'll need more answers. So during the pandemic, I wrote *Business in the Digital, Online and Virtual Space* for help when the stores were closed and we had to do business strictly online. This book was a resource tool for those who needed support and more information, to create digital products and explore other outlets to continue to build their brand in spite of the pandemic. This was a supplemental book to assist business owners, especially small business owners, to stay afloat. I wrote this book in a way to transcend any of the times that we are in now or can face in the future. Hopefully, these strategies, products and services can be incorporated in daily operational aspects of any industry business and brand. I encourage you to write your book from an approach of being timely but not to time out and be outdated just in case the season shifts or pivots again. No matter the time or season, always be a resource for the reader just in case they have questions, want to contact you for additional help, need answers and you be available to meet their needs no matter what time or season they are accessing the book.

Support Actions with a Brand Book

In addition to these brand books mentioned, I have many more books that I use with my brand, and you can check them out and purchase at www.juliaroystonstore.com.

The following are a few ways and opportunities that I include in the brand book that often can lead people to my brand book or to my brand, period.

My Calendar — How can people have a conversation with me? Go to the link www.talkwithroyston.com and schedule a call.

Email List — When you schedule an appointment, you can also opt-in to get on my email list. I send out a monthly newsletter with information, new releases, events, opportunities for training, etc.

Magazine

The Book Business Boss Magazine is a free magazine and included in the publishing package for all authors. Their ad in the magazine gives them promotional opportunities, and those who review the magazine are able to see what all we publish, read articles of interest and attend upcoming events (in-person or virtual) as a lead to work with us and build the brand.

Live Events

I cannot tell you how many live events I have hosted or attended that have led to people becoming my clients. Some people will not get to the brand book until they meet you first. I know we're talking about writing a brand book and it's important, but just writing that book alone won't do to build a sustainable and profitable brand. If you need help, let's talk: www.talkwithroyston.com. Let's go!

Virtual Events

This was our lifeline to the outside world and to continue getting our books, businesses and brands in front of new audiences during the height of the pandemic via virtual events. Even at the writing of this book, that is still a way to get your book and brand in front of new audiences via virtual events. I believe that some actions won't be going away anytime soon and hosting, participating in and helping to promote a virtual event is one good way to lead people to you.

Podcast/Media Opportunity

"Live Your Best Life" has been on the air since 2019. I had no idea I would be on Internet radio that long, but it has been a good way to lead people to me. The radio station is International and currently heard in 32 countries. Having a brand book that goes along with my show has been key as well. It is a two-way communication in that the book leads people to the show and the show leads people to my books, business and brand. Podcasts and radio shows are work! Let me say that again, "IT IS WORK!" If you are not willing to work or have the time for it or can incorporate the time, money and effort in your life, don't do it. Creating my shows and events are now a part of my life and I don't mean that in a light way. I am truly telling you that it is now a part of my life. I am creating new shows and events all of the time and looking at how I can incorporate my authors, businesses, friends, family and other people I meet into the brand of my show. It's not impossible, but it is work. On the other hand, there are rewards to the work that we put in. People recognize me, and I am able to

interview some incredible people. It is a humbling and wonderful opportunity for me and my brand, business and books. As you can tell, anything you create should have the primary purpose to work hand in hand to lead people from that event or occasion to your book, business and brand. Keep that in your mind when you create anything: eBook, paperback book, flyer, postcard or business card. How will what I have created lead people to me, my business and brand?

Social Media

Business, brands and social media go together. I did a talk recently where I told the business owners in the room that social media should be a part of your business operations, but it shouldn't be your boss. It shouldn't be the sole determiner of what you do, how you move and what you produce in your business. It should be an accompaniment or an additive to your branding and promotional plan. But, you should have a social media presence always — even if it is limited to encouraging posts, new product posts, event posts, etc. You should be online somewhere. As you can see from this graphic, I am leading people to my website but also offering a free download of my brand eBook, "Live Your Best Life."

The YouTube Channel graphic was to encourage people to follow my YouTube Channel, which is a part of my BK Royston Publishing brand. The YouTube channel has videos of events and my Sunday morning live pre-show, and always offers my brand books to bring people to my brand. All of these social media campaigns and efforts are to drive traffic toward me and my brand. Remember that should be one of your main goals with all of your efforts including meeting people on the street is to drive people to your brand through a book, social media, event or an impromptu conversation.

The Book Business Boss

I am currently in the writing stages for this book, which is the last brand of mine that I don't have an accompanying book. I have a show on Tuesdays on www.envision-radio.com called "The Book Business Boss Show," and I need a brand book to go along with it. The show gives a lot of tips, resources and tools for books, business and how to be a boss, but in this new book, I want to focus on the mindset you should have, moves you should make and the momentum you don't want to lose if you can help it.

What Type of Book Does Your Brand Need?

I have talked about my brand books that accompany my business of writing, publishing, promotion, product creation and business building. These books have come from actual client requests and business needs. What type of book does our brand need? What are some questions that your current clients or potential clients have asked repeatedly? Remember that your clients or people you meet will tell you what they want or need or a problem that they need you to solve. That's how I realized that the books that I mentioned were necessary because people kept asking me the same questions or needing help with the same problems, or I saw a gap in the market for that particular book, idea or solution. As much as we love to do what we're passionate about in business and the old saying "If you do what you love, you'll never work a day in your life" is true, but if no one buys what you love, your budget will be depleted, and you will go out of business very soon unless you change or add to your thing that you love some of the things that people need and want.

So if you're in real estate, does you book need to be a checklist of the information or documentation that your client will need to move forward with buying a property? Are there worksheets to determine how much house someone wants versus how much money they will need to put down or other calculations that go along with the real estate business?

If you're a life or health coach, do your clients need a journal, workbook, planner or other materials to go along with your sessions, retreat, conference or VIP Day?

If you're an executive or personal chef or nutritionist, do you need a cookbook or other meal planning book to accompany your client sessions for them to take home or use when they are in the grocery store or even ordering online?

I can't cover every industry in this book, but you can apply your business or industry to any of these ideas, but here's my final example. What if you're in the beauty business and want to provide style ideas, tips, etc., to your clients that are the basics and then lead them to your YouTube channel for more specifics on styling, healthy options for skin types or clothing for certain body types.

Over the next few pages, I want you to think about your business, your clients and their needs and what type of brand book that you need to create to meet your clients' needs and wants or to help solve their problems. Let's go!

What is your business?

What have your potential/current clients asked for help with in regard to your business? If you don't know, ask them or ask social media.

What are a few problems that your clients need solved or pain points that arise with your clients?

What type of brand book do you think would be best for your client? Instructional book, planner, journal, workbook or other?

_____

_____

_____

_____

_____

_____

_____

_____

_____

_____

_____

_____

_____

_____

_____

Notes:

Notes:

Brand Book Outline

A few years ago, I asked an author what the key to writing her books had been and she said an outline. I had used an outline in some of my books but not with all of my books. When I first started writing, it was strictly inspirational, or an idea came to me and then I wrote. God would say, "Write this or that." I would do it, but as time went on, there were books that needed to be written for my clients and business. I am a person of faith so I believe that God works through people and can bring inspiration in a multitude of ways. No matter how the idea or request for a specific topic is to be covered, I now make an outline. I want to make sure that I cover the topics or questions that are necessary for that particular book topic and its potential audience. I am a creative so I can get tons of ideas but if I get too many ideas, I can easily get off course and not complete anything. After 88 books, I can make an outline while I write the book which I am doing right now. Why? Because new topics come to my brain while I am writing but if it is not on topic or related or deemed necessary for this book, I will put it in another document and write about it at another time or in another book.

So with any of my writing clients, we start with the first seven questions before we write:

Topic: What do you want to write about?

Audience: Who are you writing to?

Audience level of expertise: Introduction, Intermediate or Advanced

Format: What format do you want this book to be in? Non-fiction, fiction, children's, poetry, inspirational, journal, planner or workbook or combination?

Following: Do you speak to this audience already?

Social Media: How active are you on social media?

The Offer: What are you going to offer this audience after they read the book?

Take a moment and answer those seven questions, right here and right now.

Topic: What do you want to write about?

Audience: Who are you writing to?

Audience level of expertise:

Format: What format do you want this book to be in? Non-fiction, fiction, children's, poetry, inspirational, journal, planner or workbook or combination?

_____
_____
_____
_____
_____
_____
_____
_____
_____
_____
_____
_____

Following: Do you speak to this audience already?

Social Media: How active are you on social media?

_____
_____
_____
_____
_____
_____
_____
_____
_____
_____
_____
_____
_____
_____
_____

The Offer: What are you going to offer this audience after they read the book?

Notes:

Notes:

Now that you have the topic, the audience, the format, following and social media, we need to determine exactly what you want to include in your brand book. What do you want to cover?

Here are some options:

- ➢ The back story of your life and what you have learned that gives you credibility and accountability to lead others to want to work with you more closely?
- ➢ A step-by-step instructional book that can potentially be used for a workbook/textbook?
- ➢ Five to ten principles that you have developed as your approach to your

business or the foundational standards that drives your business?
➢ A book that solves a problem or answers a question.

On the next page, our next steps are to develop an actual outline of 5–10 things that you want to include in your book.

Topic 1:

_____

_____

_____

_____

Topic 2:

_____

_____

_____

_____

Topic 3:

_____

_____

_____

_____

Topic 4:

_____
_____
_____
_____

Topic 5:

_____
_____
_____
_____

Topic 6:

_____
_____
_____
_____

Topic 7:

_____
_____
_____
_____

Topic 8:

_____
_____
_____
_____

Topic 9:

_____
_____
_____
_____

Topic 10:

_____

_____

_____

_____

These main topics are now your outline and now, just like in high school, it's time to fill in the additional resources or information that you want to include in the book under each subtopic.

Some writing guidelines are:
- ❖ Do not be concerned about how long each chapter should be but focus on the information you want to include and the questions that you want to answer.

- ❖ It doesn't matter where you start on the outline, just start where you start until you finish.
- ❖ Strive to write every single day even if it is for 20 minutes a day so that you can finish.
- ❖ Finally, it doesn't matter whether you use a desktop computer, laptop computer, write in a journal with a pen or pencil or speak it in a phone, just write.

Notes:

The Look of the Book

Now that you've been writing, it's time to also plan out the vision for the physical or electronic version of the book itself. Think about the interior and the cover of the book as well. The book's cover is the face of the book and what people will notice first even before the title of the book. Not only should the book cover be attractive, but it also needs to make sense and connect with the interior of the book. The book cover and interior topic should agree. Taking this idea to the next level, remember that you are striving to draw people to you and your brand. So as much brand clarity as possible should be put into the thought processes of the creation of the book's cover. If people are confused by your book and book cover, they may not be willing to work with you especially if the sole purpose of your business is to improve, clarify or rectify a problem with someone's business or life. The thought would be, "how can they help me when they need to help themselves with this book?" I am not striving to be harsh but honest and save you some heartache when the cover makes perfect sense to you, but your audience docsn't get it and more importantly accept it. I've changed many covers because it wasn't clear with the audience that I was trying to reach, work with and receive payment from. It is terrible.

Consider this, does the cover need to be designed with your brand colors or does that matter?

If the book is about you and your story, do you need to grace the cover of the book or no?

What is a symbol, emblem or logo that goes along with your brand that should somehow be visual on the front or back of your book cover?

Should there be room for discussion questions or room for people to write inside the book?

If the book is a memoir book or one that tells a chronological story, should the journal, planner or workbook be separate from the main book or no? Something to think about, if the journal, planner or workbook is separate, it can be sold alone or as a set. More products, more profits. Just a thought…

With that being said, remember that you have to consider your topic, industry and where you want the reader/audience/client to connect with you and do business with you in the future. Also, if you don't know, you need to ask your clients/audience how they want to work on this topic, assignment or project. Do they want a digital planner, or do they want to work with a physical paper item or an electronic book with links to videos, audio or other electronic materials?

If you have worked with people before and it was a pleasant experience, don't hesitate to ask them for references, endorsements or testimonials about their experience. Keep their comments in a separate document and you can include it in your book at the beginning of the book or on the back of the book cover. You can use these comments on your landing page or website under, "what people are saying," or "testimonial" or "what people think about our services." These same endorsements, testimonials can be used on any promotional social media posts, graphic or other promotional materials. I am all about repurposing content that will support, lead or drive traffic to you, your business and brand. The book should be no different and it should be presented in a way that people would want to know more, grow with and work with you!

This is my personal opinion, but if you choose to have a foreword or endorsement inside or on the back of your book, make sure that the person is really willing to endorse or in some way support your book. Will they record a short video? Will they be interviewed on your social media platforms? Will they purchase or sponsor so many for their audience or followers? Will they host an event on their platform or at their venue? Their name and words on a page are wonderful and help as an endorsement, but if it doesn't transfer into dollars, their words look great on paper and carry little weight. Also, remember that you want a foreword from someone who is an influencer and not just your family and friends who want their name on a book without sharing with a broader audience that the author cannot access. If your family or friends are influencers as well, it's an even better opportunity for you and their brand. Be sure to make the opportunity a win/win situation and not just one sided. If they assist you in this endeavor, be sure and offer the same or similar or equal level of assistance for them, their business or brand.

If you the author or business owner has access to that same audience, why do you need the/their endorsement unless it will expand or extend your reach. Think about it before you ask for a foreword or endorsement.

If you need help, schedule a conversation at www.talkwithroyston.com.

Notes:

The End Game

The other difference in writing a brand book vs. any other book is the audience's call to action or the 'end game' of the book. Where do you want people to go and/or what do you want people to do after or while reading your book?

This is a totally different thought process from a fiction, children's, poetry, memoir, etc., genre of book. Remember that your brand is the focus and has the potential to grow, expand and soar into the next level. Throughout the entire process of reading this book, the follow-up and execution of writing your own brand book, keep that in mind. Also, as an additional thought, with relationship to your brand, always be thinking about how anything will impact it: no matter the investment, audience or location. We are talking about writing a brand book but even if you are writing an article, pamphlet, blog post, email message, social media post or comment, think about how it can have the potential to affect your brand. Hopefully, you'll think twice before you press send, submit or comment.

With the "End Game" game in mind, where do you want them to go, visit or engage with your platform, social media or website after or during reading your brand book? See the examples in the previous chapter to see what your brand has to offer already or create one or more of these opportunities for your brand book to be a part of or connected to or lead people to want to participate in one or more of your upcoming events, trainings or opportunities to do business. Review this list to see what services or opportunities to engage your audience that already have in place or need to create.

Lead Magnet
Email List
Discovery Call
Sales Call
Free Download
Coaching
Mentoring
Workshop
Course
Videos
Live Event
Virtual Event
Podcast/Media Opportunity

You know if you need help, let's have a conversation at www.talkwithroyston.com.

In the past, it was advised to have a separate social media page for each book or a separate website for each book but I really advise that you have an Internet headquarters or website to have all of your access points in one place. If I had it to do all over again, I would have established an umbrella company that would encompass all of my businesses. I still can do that and may do that one day. In the meantime, I am encouraging you to think as big as possible and not limit yourself. With that said, do you have the headquarters established for your business, this book and beyond? The headquarters is a website, landing page or at least a bio link page for people to engage with. An example, www.juliaakroyston.com, is my bio link page but it links to all of my websites and online stores.

Here's an example of a landing page, https://www.bookbusinessbosses.com/bookbossinfo.html.

Examples of my website are www.bkroystonpublishing.com or www.juliaroyston.net.

My online stores are www.juliaroystonstore.com, www.roystonchildrenbookstore.com and www.roystonroyalbookstore.com.

Are your systems in place for people to work with you beyond the book? Where do you want people to go to next after your book? What are the next steps?

Do you have a calendar for people to schedule an appointment with you in addition to your email and/or phone number? I have consistently shown you throughout this book my calendar link so that you can very easily schedule a conversation. Besides your perspective on a particular topic or industry profession or service, driving traffic to you is second only to the topic.

Once people get on your mailing list, do you have a monthly, quarterly or bi-annual newsletter or check-in communication that you send or plan to send via email? While they are on your list, you may want to schedule an on-demand webinar or event for them to sign up for whether it's paid or free. People can always opt-out of your email list once they get on it and get connected to you, but the brand book can be the door, introduction or pathway for people to begin, continue and be lifelong clients of yours.

Be sure to include your social media platforms and website on everything or as much real estate in the brand book as possible. People may purchase your book in person or online but before they take it to the next level, they may watch you for months or even years before they come in closer and want to work with you more. There are people who connect with you immediately through your brand book and want to work with you right away, and we love that, but there are others who take some time to get to know you and then want to work with you.

Thus, make sure that your brand book is rich in content, beautifully formatted with an appealing layout and then have ways intentionally included for people to contact you when they're ready.

The brand book represents you, your business and your brand. The brand book is your intellectual property, make good use of it.

About the Author

Julia Royston spends her days doing what she loves, writing, publishing, speaking and coaching others to write and monetize their messages to the world.

"Helping You Get Your Message to the Masses and Turn Your Words into Wealth" is her why and motto. To date, Julia has written 85+ books, published 400+, recorded three music CDs and coached more than 250 to turn books into businesses. She is the owner of five companies, a non-profit organization, editor of the *Book Business Boss Magazine* as well as the host of "Live Your Best Life," heard each Sunday morning at 10:00 a.m. EST and the "Book Business Boss Show" on Tuesdays at 10:30 a.m. EST on www.envision-radio.com, and a contributing author to *Envision Radio Magazine*. To stay connected with Julia, visit www.juliaakroyston.com.

Other Books by Julia Royston

www.ingramcontent.com/pod-product-compliance
Lightning Source LLC
Chambersburg PA
CBHW071224160426
43196CB00012B/2410